A FIRESIDE BOOK

PUBLISHED

BY SIMON &

SCHUSTER

NEW YORK

LONDON

TORONTO

SYDNEY

TOKYO

SINGAPORE

THE TAO OF

BASEBALL

Gō

FIRESIDE
Simon & Schuster Building
Rockefeller Center
1230 Avenue of the Americas
New York, New York 10020

Designed by Bonni Leon
Manufactured in the United States of America

10   9   8   7   6   5   4   3   2   1

Library of Congress Cataloging-in-Publication Data
Gō
    The tao of baseball/Gō.
        p.   cm.
    "A Fireside book."
    1. Baseball.   2. Taoism.   I. Title.
GV867.3.G6   1991
796.357—dc20   91-8879   CIP
ISBN 0-671-70430-3

ACKNOWLEDGMENTS

Since there is no real beginning, there is also no real end to my gratitude for the help I receive along the Way.

I should, nevertheless, like to acknowledge and thank the team at Fireside and Simon & Schuster, especially my battery mate, Ed Walters, for his knowledge of the hitters and for calling a good game. Also, I wish to thank my agent, Philip Spitzer, for giving me a shot at the Show. Thanks also to my Mother and Father, and brother, Donald, who initiated me into the way of baseball. Thanks, of course, to D.

And finally, I'd like to thank my wife, Marie-Claire. Words will never be enough.

Gō

A B O O K F O R

PLAYERS,
MANAGERS,
UMPIRES,
AND FANS

A Player is someone who plays the Game.

A Manager is someone who directs
the way Players play the Game.

An Umpire is someone who governs the
Game.

A Fan is someone who watches the Game.

One man can be Many.

CONTENTS

The Origin of This Book   11

INTRODUCING THE TAO   13

THE TAO OF PLAY   33

THE COMMENTARIES   115

THE TAO OF BASEBALL   151

T H E
O R I G I N
O F   T H I S
B O O K

It is important that I begin this book in the beginning, so that the reader may clearly see my intentions.

It was not my intent to write this book, but when I look back upon it, it seems as though it was intended all along. In other words, I was perfect for the job, but I wasn't looking for this particular work.

One night, I was sitting still, looking at a picture I had made some time before.

This is a two-sided picture that I hung in front of a window. I would often watch it spinning and changing shapes. The picture is a representation of the Tao and the changing elements of Yin and Yang within the Tao. It is different from most pictures of the Tao because all of the Yang elements have been cut out to permit the light to shine through and represent them.

Now, at some point I saw, superimposed in my mind, a baseball in the same attitude as the Yin-Yang symbol.

At one moment, no connection. In the next moment, connection.

Now knowing a little about the Tao and a little about baseball, I began to see images overlapping and connecting in my mind. One moment, nothing; the next moment, something.

This is how this book began. Everything that follows has its origins in this simple connection.

INTRODUCING

THE TAO

THE TAO OF THE
INTRODUCTION

There are many readers who will come to this never having heard the word *Tao* before, or who may have heard it somewhere but are not really certain as to what it means. Let me start out by defining it in my own Way.

Many of you may think that the Tao is an ancient religion from China. If you think that the Tao is in geography, then you have not yet seen the world; and if you think that the Tao is in history, then you do not yet know the time; and if you think that the Tao is in religion, then you do not yet have faith. It is true, however, that the Tao is an ancient religion from China.

It would be more accurate to call it an ancient science. This is not to say that the Tao is an ancient science, merely that man studies the Tao as though it were a science, because it is the most efficacious Way of understanding and imparting the complete reality of life.

The study of the Tao is not like a conventional science, where a man can analyze and measure; it is not theoretical and it cannot be proven to exist. The Tao allows man to behave in these ways, but it is not the path to the real Tao, merely an acknowledgment of the obvious. The real Tao is the science of remembering who we are. It is not a matter of making the world conform to our views, but it is rather a matter of making our views conform to the world. This is why it is said that the study of the Tao is a reversion and not a progression. Reversion is a progression in a backward way.

Most of what I say here may seem self-evident. It is, once you understand it, but when you understand it, chances are that you will see that you have never thought about it before. So how could you have understood it? This is my point. There is a beauty and perfection to the world, a mysterious guiding force at play in ourselves and all around us. The Ancestors have referred to this greatness as the Tao, or to translate into English, as the Way. "The Way," if used often enough, will begin to accumulate the same depth of meaning as "the Tao" had for the Ancestors. In other words, the word will of itself define itself by itself, and you will be able to understand what it means, or more simply, you will know. Even words such as *birth* and *God* are greatly misunderstood because of neglect.

It is quite natural that everything conform to the Tao or Way, since everything is under its domain. It was here before everything; and will be here after everything. It is not a creation of man, but rather the Creator of man. The word *Tao* points to a recognition of the Source of all things and the harmony within all of its manifestations. It was an attempt to explain the unexplainable, and a way of pointing out the greatness of all things in a time when we had, as we have today, forgotten the essential meaning and mystery of life. It is a word that names the unnameable.

When you begin to study the words that the Ancestors have passed down about the Tao, you will find them paradoxical and contradictory. This is why the Tao is funny and serious at the same time. It makes sense, and yet it is nonsense. When you try to talk about it, you have nothing to say; when you give up trying to talk about it, you can't shut up. Only there is nothing you can say about it. Please consider this carefully.

There are many who wish to study the Tao. There is no school large enough nor any man foolish enough to try to teach it. There are a few who can point out its direction and the best way of getting there, but it can only be learned alone, from within. If you want to teach children about the wind, take them to a hilltop.

The Tao is the teacher and the Tao teaches through living. If you want to learn about the Tao, look to the Tao; the Tao is all around you and yet it appears to be nowhere to be found. When you ask a question, you will find it has already been answered.

The only condition the Tao has made permanent is that we must be who we are. In this we have no choice. Whether we accept this reality or reject it is a matter of personal choice. Personal choice is, after all, also part of the Tao. Upon close examination, however, there is really nothing to choose, because we already are who we are. This is why we should not take ourselves too seriously. It makes it easier to accept that, in the Tao of all things, we are just one tiny part.

There are some who will say that when I talk about the Tao, I am talking about God. There are times when you could translate the Tao as God and it would make perfect sense. There are times when it would make perfect nonsense as in "The God of Baseball." This is why it is best left as the Way, "The Way of Baseball."

Which brings us full circle. This book is a presentation of the Tao of baseball, and it is my understanding of the Tao of baseball. It is by no means the final word on the Tao of baseball. Anyone who considers it carefully will be able to increase and develop its explanations. The only real limit to understanding the Tao is time.

But don't worry. The Tao can be embraced in less than a fraction of a second. Just don't take forever to do it.

It is my intent that this book will in some way transcend the realm of baseball and approach the vastness of life. Since it is the Tao that guides all things, it is natural that something such as baseball be created according to the laws of the Tao. By pointing out this simple reality, may we gain a further understanding of the Tao in the law of life.

The Year of the Horse (A.D. 1990)

T H E
INTRODUCTION
OF THE TAO

Before we begin with the new, we must first divest ourselves of the old.

A very long time ago, in the twilight of our innocence and the dawn of our concern, an Ancient set out to find the Way back to the Source of All Things.

At first he traveled the Way of People until he came to the source of Mankind.

Then he traveled the Way of the Earth until he came to the source of Nature.

Then he traveled the Way of the Heavens until he came to the source of the Universe.

Then he traveled the Way of the Heart until he came to the source of Love.

And finally he traveled the Way of his Being until he came to the Source of All Things.

And here he saw that all Ways were part of one great never-ending Way to the Source. All creation flowed out of and flowed back to the Source along one infinite Way. Everything was a part of it; nothing could escape it. Every Way was unique and self-sustaining and perfect unto itself, and yet every Way was connected to and a fraction of the whole Way.

He also saw that men no longer knew that they were part of the Great Way of All Things.

And when he had returned to this world, he was by then an old man.

At complete peace and at one with the Great Way, he headed for the mountains to pass his remaining time until his return to the Source, but no sooner had he begun than a young man stumbled upon him and asked of him the secret of the Great Way to the Source.

And so he passed on his knowledge and sent the young man on his Way, and when the young man turned to thank the wise old Ancient, he had disappeared without a trace from the face of this world.

And in the same way, from generation to generation, the Ancients handed down their knowledge of the Great Way of All Things, until this present day, this present moment in fact. Only in the language of the Ancients, the Great Way was called the Tao.

In ancient times it was written with the symbols of a left foot stopping and starting and a head:

In modern times it is written as:

There are two Ways you can write this in English, the old Way, Tao, or the new Way, Dao. Whichever Way you write it, it should be pronounced something like Dao or Dow. But since many of us have started out with the old Way of Tao, many of us will finish with the old Way of Tao. The important thing is to understand what the Ancients meant.

YIN AND YANG
MADE MANIFEST

Chances are that even if you have never heard of the Tao before, you may have heard of Yin and Yang, or may have seen this symbol:

It is essential, if you are to come to an understanding of the Tao of baseball, that you first come to an understanding of the Yin and Yang of baseball. Without Yin and Yang, there couldn't even be a game.

In the very beginning there wasn't even nothing.
And in the very end there won't even be nothing.
No game, no nothing.

Where did the universe come from?
Where will the universe go to?
What were you before you were born?
What will you be after you die?
There is not even an answer.
Anything you can say just ain't it.

The Ancients referred to the Source of All Things as the Tao, and the original state they named Wu Chi, the Ultimate Nothing, the Big Zero, the Infinite No-Nothing-None. The first map of reality the Ancients handed down was thus

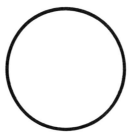

a circle.

It was the state of oneness, the void, the all, the cosmic womb. It was eternal, infinite, perfect, and complete beyond all knowledge.

It was the Tao. It was the light before the dark, the silence before the sound, the bliss before the concern, the rest before the change, the life before the death, the female before the male, the summer before the winter, the nothing before the something, the win before the loss.

And then, simultaneously, Bang! Everything changed.
The universe and everything in it was created.
Play ball indeed!

And so was born creation.
The Tao remained the Tao, but the state of Creation the Ancients named T'ai Chi, the Fat Ultimate, the Cosmic Roof-Beam. The second map that the Ancients handed down was thus

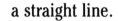 a straight line.

It represented the law of two, the order of change, the balance of nature, the rules of the game. It was the light and the dark, the heavens and the earth, the male and the female, the silence and the sound, the rest and the change, the birth and the death, the summer and the winter, the young and the old, the here and the there, the something and the nothing, the perceiver and the perceived, the positive and the negative, the win and the loss.

And the Ancients, the more they looked, the more they saw, until they had seen enough. It was always, no matter where you looked, going to be one or the other, positive or negative, up or down, and that without the one there couldn't be the other.

And the third map that the Ancients handed down was thus a combination of the two;

and the one part they named Yang and the other part Yin.

Now in ancient times Yang, or The Light or The Sun's Out or The Out in the Open, was written as

with a mound with steps on it to show the higher meaning, and with the sun and either its rays or a flag waving brightly in the wind. It represented the positive force, the male, the heavens, the up, the light, the birth, the summer, the young, the here, the win.

And Yin, or Now It Is Cloudy, or It's Dark Out, was written as

with the same mound, the symbol for Now, and vapor forming into clouds. It was the negative force, the female, the earth, the down, the dark, the winter, the death, the old, the there, the loss.

Each was necessary for the other. Each was created from the other. Each was in the other. Each would become the other. Each, however, seeking out the Original Tao, the Source, trying to blend the one into the other into the All, but held in place by its very Existence, enhancing and accumulating despite itself, waiting until the time of return. The fourth map the Ancients handed down was thus:

T H E
O R I G I N
OF   THE
BASEBALL

And so it has come to me, while knowing a little about baseball and a little about the Tao, that the baseball, in its construction, is a perfect three-dimensional representation of the Tao and the Yin-Yang principle as handed down by the Ancestors.

The baseball is pure Tao. It is the tao of the Tao. It is Yin and Yang manifested as one. It is simple. It is spherical. It is perfect.

It is tangible. It is the essence of the game. A bat alone is a stick. The bat only becomes essential once you have a baseball to hit. A baseball alone is still a baseball.

How the first ball was inspired is almost lost to time. The baseball, however, historically owes a great deal of its inspiration to the British cricket ball, whose weight and circumference are practically identical, but which possesses one straight seam.

The baseball uniquely gives the illusion of having two seams, and we even speak of a four-seamed fastball, but in reality there is only one continuous, serpentine seam. If you run your finger along it, it will end up back at the beginning, never having left the ball.

A baseball is constructed from two pieces of cowhide (today), or horsehide (yesterday), in the shape of an elongated eight. Turned upon its side, each piece is reminiscent of the symbol of infinity.

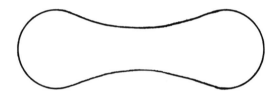

These two pieces are then wrapped and tightly sewn with 108 stitches around a core of cork and rubber that has been bound by lengths of coarse and fine yarn. The core can be viewed as an expression of the Tao, representing the center, the beginning, the oneness of everything, the inner, the perfection. The yarn becomes a means of connecting the inner with the outer, a padding out, meat on the bones. It is the organs, the nerves, an infinity of fiber communicating the internal to the external, the external to the internal. When the two halves of hide are sewn over the whole, they complete the inner with the outer, protecting the inside or spirit from the outside forces of the world, much as the body houses the spirit. And all baseballs, the Spaldings and the kids' balls alike, if used often enough, will eventually lose their covers, and their yarn will unravel to reveal a small, compact core. This corresponds to the eventual deterioration of the body into its Source, the earth. A baseball is made of earthly matter, as are we. But that core remains. It could be rewrapped or remade into a new ball. The core, like the spirit of the game, will always be there, awaiting new arms, new gloves, new bats, awaiting a new day to be put into play.

Now one of the halves or hemispheres used to make the baseball can represent Yang,

and the other Yin,

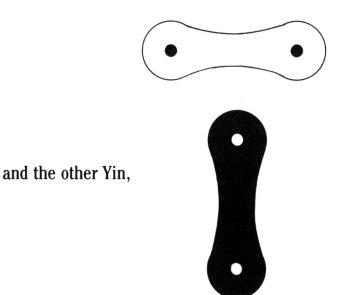

and their union around the spirit or core creates a life within Life, a force within Forces, the tao within the Tao, imbued with the possibilities of expression in terms of the fundamental laws of Yin and Yang. And like all of creation, no two baseballs are alike, both in their form and in their history: pitchers will discard some because of their feel, others they will scuff to modify their function; some will be historic and occupy Cooperstown, others will be delegated as practice balls; some will be autographed souvenirs, some will be in use at this moment.

Baseballs are not capable of awareness, although in a very strange way they are alive since we have created them. They are extensions of ourselves and of our world uniquely held together in the Tao of man against man in the game we call baseball.

THE TAO
OF PLAY

GŌ'S FIRST LAW:

YIN + YANG = TAO

The purest example of the dualities inherent in the Tao of baseball is the relationship of the Yang of winning and the Yin of losing. Everything within the Tao of baseball will abide by this rule of duality.

Since we view winning as being good or "the objective," this is usually represented as Yang, and since we view losing as being bad, or "the nonobjective," this will be represented as Yin. This does not mean to say that Yang is good and that Yin is bad; only that in the context of the game, we have created a duality—between winning and losing—and that the attributes of this duality conform to the laws of the Tao.

Taken together, the two create the Tao of the game, or to put it another way, the game is completed when the winner and the loser have been determined.

Like the baseball itself, the game of baseball contains dualities that conform to the laws of the Tao:

There is the firm force Yang;
There is the yielding force Yin.
They are held together by Time within the Tao.

Without the Firm, there is not the Yielding;
Without the Yielding, there is not the Firm.
The Firm changes to the Yielding;
The Yielding changes to the Firm.

This is how the Tao holds them together with Time.

The Firm creates the Yielding;
The Yielding creates the Firm.
The Firm opposes the Yielding;
The Yielding opposes the Firm.
Thus as they oppose, they create at the same Time.
This is why the Tao is beyond Time.

For example:

There is the Yang of fair;
There is the Yin of foul,

Creating the Tao of the Field of Play.

There is the Yang of offense;
There is the Yin of defense,
Creating the Tao of the Opposition.

There is the Yang of the hitter;
There is the Yin of the pitcher,
Creating the Tao of the At Bat.

There is the Yang of more runs;
There is the Yin of fewer runs,
Creating the Tao of the Score.

There is the Yang of the top of the first;
There is the Yin of the bottom of the ninth,
Creating the Tao of a Regulation Game.

There is the Yang of umpires;
There is the Yin of the plays,
Creating the Tao of Officiating.

There is the Yang of winning;
There is the Yin of losing,
Creating the Tao of the Game.

There is the Yang of home games;
There is the Yin of away games,
Creating the Tao of the Schedule.

There is the Yang of Opening Day;
There is the Yin of the last game of the World Series,
Creating the Tao of the Season.

There is the Yang of the manager;
There is the Yin of the players,
Creating the Tao of the Team.

There is the Yang of the players;
There is the Yin of the fans,
Creating the Tao of the Sport.

There is the Yang of the Major Leagues;
There is the Yin of the Minor Leagues,
Creating the Tao of the Career.

There is the Yang of the National League;
There is the Yin of the American League,
Creating the Tao of the Major Leagues.

There is the Yang of owners;
There is the Yin of managers and players,
Creating the Tao of the Business of Baseball.

There is the Yang of the League;
There is the Yin of the owners, managers, and players,
Creating the Tao of the Politics of Baseball.

There is the Yang of American Baseball;
There is the Yin of International Baseball,
Creating the Tao of Global Baseball.

THE TAO AS COMMON GROUND

or Manifestations of Yin and Yang

The Tao supports all things and looks after all things.

It is there all around us, and we are suspended in it like puppets on a string.

It nourishes from below in the earth and protects from on high in the sky.

The Tao is the common ground of all things. You will find it underlying and overlying all things.

It is an arrangement of order that enables all things to find their way in this universe.

If the Tao is below you, then you must be above it, and if the Tao is above you, then you must be below it.

Thus the Tao underlies and overlies all things. It manifests itself through change or action. Change or action is manifested in elements of Yin and Yang.

To test, I cite:

The field underlies the play and is the Tao of Place;
What is happening upon it is manifested as Yin and Yang.

The bases overlie the field and are the Tao of the Path;
Who is on them and when they are on them is manifested as Yin
and Yang.

The strike zone overlies home plate and is the Tao of the Target;
Where the ball crosses it is manifested as Yin and Yang.

The bat overlies the strike zone and is the Tao of Advancement;
How the bat prevents the ball from crossing it is manifested as Yin
and Yang.

The rules underlie the game and are the Tao of Order;
What they decree is manifested as Yin and Yang.

The umpire overlies the rules and is the Tao of Judgment;
What he calls is manifested as Yin and Yang.

The pitcher overlies the pitcher's mound and is the Tao of the
    Enactment;
What he enacts is manifested as Yin and Yang.

The ball underlies the game and is the Tao of Baseball;
What is done to it and where it goes are manifested as Yin and
    Yang.

The moment overlies the game and is the Tao of Destiny;
How we react to it is manifested as Yin and Yang.

THE TAO
OF THE
PLAYING
FIELD

Without the infinite, there could not be the finite. Therefore, without an acceptance of the infinity (or timelessness) of the Tao, the game would have no finite end. Creating the duality of a winner and a loser also creates the need for an end to the game, to be determined by a formal acceptance of the infinity of the Tao.

It has therefore been determined that three strikes would make an out, to eliminate an endless attempt at hitting the ball; four balls a walk, to prevent a ceaseless parade of wild pitches; there would be three outs to an inning; and nine innings to a complete game—or extra innings until a victor is determined. Without this standard, no game would ever finish and nothing—according to the laws of duality—would have been achieved.

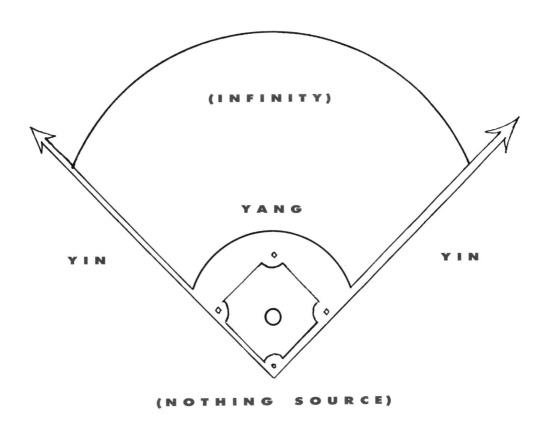

(INFINITY)

YANG

YIN   YIN

(NOTHING SOURCE)

The baseball playing field is a perfect structure of the Tao.
Starting at the Source or nothing, one proceeds into infinity.
Yang is fair.
Yin is foul.

A player becomes an expression of the Tao when he runs from the Source or nothingness of home into the infinite Tao. Again, bowing down to the infinite, and to prevent players from running into the sunset, ninety feet was deemed a perfectly adequate distance, and infinity was thus expressed in a straight circle or diamond of 360 feet. (Note that the circle also is graded into 360 degrees.)

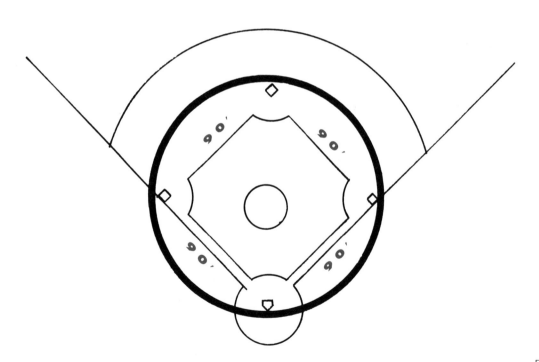

Offensively, Yang augments the farther the ball is hit away from home plate and diminishes the closer the ball is hit to home plate.

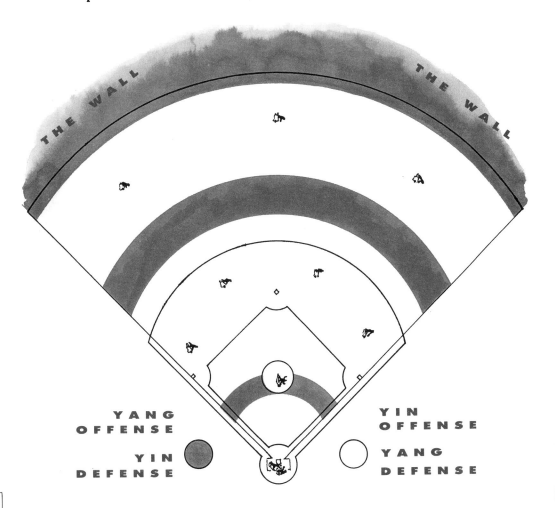

It is the reverse of the defensive field of play. Specifically, the field can be divided into three increasing degrees of Yang and three increasing degrees of Yin, corresponding to the fielders' positions. The area of greatest Yang is the wall and over, followed by a smaller area between the outfielders and the infielders, followed by the smallest area of Yang between the infielders and the catcher.

When viewed as a cross section, the outfield becomes a Yin-on-Yang sandwich, and the infield, a Yang-on-Yin sandwich.

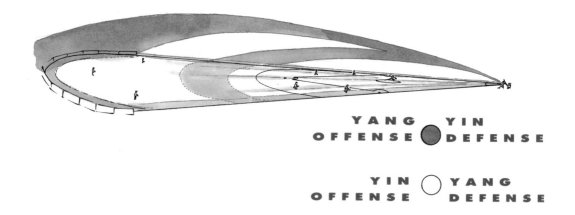

YANG YIN
OFFENSE DEFENSE

YIN YANG
OFFENSE DEFENSE

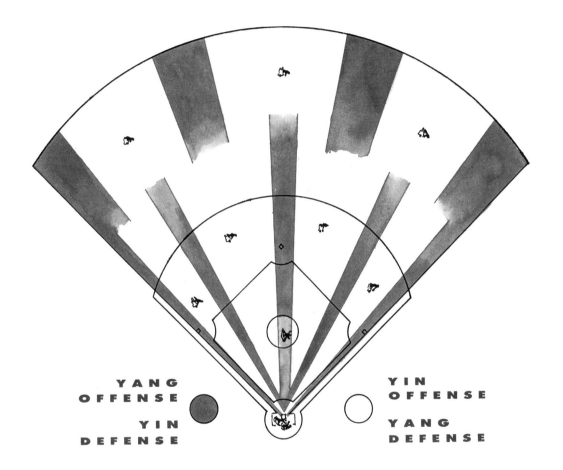

When viewed across the width of the field, the field is divided into gaps or alleys of increasing Yang, and areas of increasing Yin, corresponding to the fielders' positions.

In general, the harder the ball is hit, the wider the Yang; the softer the ball is hit, the narrower the Yang.

The lower the ball is hit, the wider the Yang; the higher the ball is hit, the narrower the Yang (with the exception of the home run).

Pop-ups and grounders in the infield are Yin and likely to be outs. Balls hit over the infielders' heads are Yang and likely to be base hits.

Fly balls in the outfield are Yin and likely to be caught. Balls hit really high in the outfield are Yang and likely to be home runs. Balls hit close to the ground are Yang and are more likely to be base hits.

Although most managers attempt to present a balance between left- and right-handed hitters in their batting order, there are still many more right-handed hitters, as well as right-handed pitchers. This leads to more balls being hit to the left side of the field, which thus becomes Yang, than to the right side of the field, which thus becomes Yin.

From a strategic viewpoint, however, left field is closer to third base and represents an easier throw to home plate, while right field is farther from third base and requires a more difficult throw

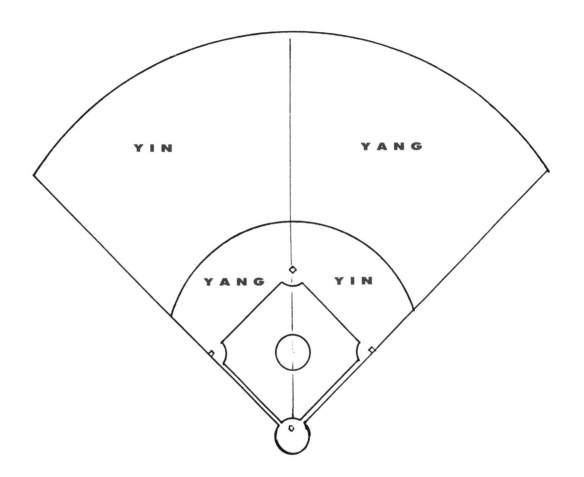

YIN YANG

YANG YIN

to home plate. The outfield thus becomes the reverse of the infield, with right field being more Yang than left field, which is more Yin.

THE TAO OF THE OUTFIELD WALL

The outfield wall is a formal recognition of the infinity of the Tao. Anyone who has ever played the outfield without a wall in sandlot baseball knows the infinity of the field. A ball sent soaring over the outfielders' heads must be chased down as the runner saunters around the bases. With the crack of the bat, the fielders will often collapse and argue as to who is going to get the ball.

Achieving the Tao with the long ball is the ultimate Yang for the hitter. He has been rewarded for his power to attain the infinite by overcoming the limits of the wall or fence. The outfielders have been spared the chase by the wall, and in many cases they are deprived of an out as well because they have run out of room. This is in recognition of the real; anything beyond *this* point is *gone.*

The wall manifests its Yang by its presence. Without the wall, hits between the outfielders would have gone for home runs. They now become triples and doubles and—should the outfielder play the carom right—a single. And where previous deep hits would have been outs, they now become home runs. The infinite is now objectively achieved, and anything short of its parameter is in play. No wall can completely separate the infinite from the finite or the Tao from the tao. The unreal can still intrude, for the wall is merely a representation and the Tao can be achieved within its limits. This we call an inside-the-park home run.

THE EIGHT
TRIGRAMS

In the beginning everything was One, everything was directly linked to the Tao. For the Ancients, there was no thought, no distinction, only a direct understanding of the Tao.

As soon as the Ancients began to examine this direct understanding of the Tao, they found themselves apart from the Tao, separated by an indirect understanding of the Tao. They entered into the realm of concern and the world of duality, or Two.

Upon examining this duality, they discovered that it was created from the same source as the Tao, and yet it consisted of opposing forces that they represented as Yin and Yang. Everything seemed to fit into this model.

Upon further examination, they discovered that from this Two had arisen more than Two, or Three. The Yang and Yin model could no longer accommodate this reality. So the Ancients represented this augmented reality with a new model based upon pairs of Yin and Yang, which could be combined into four possible pairs.

Yang	———	**Yin**	— —
Yang	———	**Yin**	— —
Yang	———	**Yin**	— —
Yin	— —	**Yang**	———

When their understanding of the Tao outgrew even this model, they expanded it to one based upon three varying elements of Yin and Yang. The model now consisted of eight possible combinations of Yin and Yang. This they represented in trigrams, with a solid line representing Yang and a broken line representing Yin. Change was introduced from the bottom and flowed upward.

The Eight Trigrams were created by the Ancients as a way of classifying the fundamental elements of the Tao. They classify according to essence as opposed to substance. This is why they should not be taken literally. They classify according to change as opposed to permanence. This is why they can be universally applied.

When examining the elements of the world, they are rendered as heaven, Chien ☰ ; earth, K'un ☷ ; thunder, Chen ☳ ; water, K'an ☵ ; mountain, Ken ☶ ; wind (wood), Sun ☴ ; fire, Li ☲ ; and lake, Tui ☱ .

When examining the elemental forces of the world, they are rendered as empowering ☰ , yielding ☷ , initiating ☳ , engulfing ☵ , silencing ☶ , penetrating ☴ , illuminating ☲ , and uplifting ☱ .

When examining the elements of the family, they are rendered as father ☰ , mother ☷ , first son ☳ , second son ☵ , third son ☶ , first daughter ☴ , second daughter ☲ , and third daughter ☱ .

When examining the elements of the human body, they are rendered as the head ☰ , the belly ☷ , the feet ☳ , the ears ☵ , the hands ☶ , the thighs ☴ , the eyes ☲ , and the mouth ☱ .

THE TAO OF
DEFENSE

The defense most closely resembles a family and can be rendered as father = pitcher ☰ , mother = catcher ☷ , first son = first baseman ☳ , second son = second baseman ☵ , third son = third baseman ☶ , first daughter = left fielder ☴ , second daughter = center fielder ☲ , and the third daughter = right fielder ☱ . The model of the trigrams responds very well with one exception: there are eight trigrams and nine men on the field!

Eight is a balanced (even) number in our world. Nine is an imbalanced (odd) number. Yin and Yang form a base of two (dualism). Anything that cannot be broken down by two will have a remaining element of either Yin or Yang, and be considered imbalanced. Upon examining this reality, some player out of the nine must be the odd man out, must be without a proper place. This man must be the shortstop (even the name suggests oddness). Every other player has a place, but the shortstop has no base and is in reality an addition, someone to cover the gap between second and third bases.

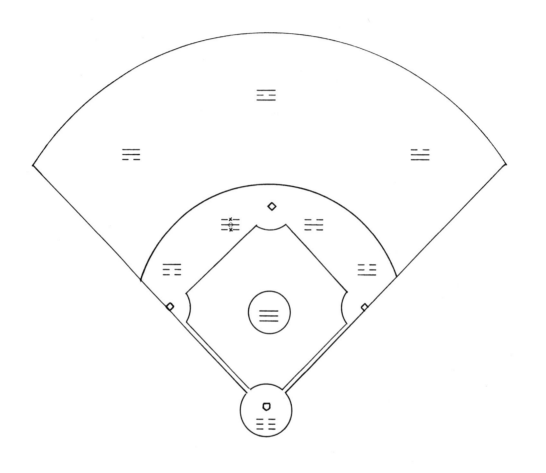

An eight-man defense or team would be more balanced, more harmonious within the game. But if you start off odd, you have to finish odd. Baseball today is imbalanced in respect to offense and defense. Defense (Yin) is more Yang than offense (Yang), and offense (Yang) is more Yin than defense (Yin). The success ratio of the defense is approximately seven out of ten. In other words, for every ten men who come to the plate, seven will become outs and three will reach base. The success ratio of the offense is approximately three out of ten in reaching base. This imbalance (assuming that a ratio of five out of ten or one out of two being balanced and where the offense would have a 50-percent chance of reaching base) can largely be attributed to the shortstop. The short-stop's role is the equivalent of having a twin for the second son (since most of his functions mirror those of the second baseman). Second base is now covered by two men, creating the possibility of the "twin killing," the double play. (There are other ways of creating the double play, but this is the most common one.) For these reasons I have indicated the shortstop as ⚏̄ , the twin. Traditionally, a solid Yang line with a circle indicates imminent change to Yin, and a broken line with an x in the middle indicates imminent change to Yang.

The Infielders

THE PITCHER, CHIEN, the Creator

The pitcher is the leader and spirit of the defense. He stands in the center at the highest point above his team on the mound, from which vantage he can clearly confront all challenges. He is the most Yang of all the defensive players. He is directly involved in every play. The entire team must respond to his direction. He is the father, the hunter, the protector, the creator. When he is balanced, he is dominating without being domineering, commanding yet at ease, working without toiling, pitching yet also fielding. He creates the work of the game. Imbalanced, he leads the entire team to defeat, working beyond his capacity, losing his control, and beating himself in the habitual. Due to the stress and demand of the responsibilities, it is the only position to be represented with an array of starters and relievers, nine to ten men, who can take over at the slightest sign of weakening. Offensively, he is the opposite, extreme Yin. He is the head of the defense.

☷ THE CATCHER, K'UN, the Receiver

The catcher stands at the heart and is at the lowest point of the defense. He protects the last refuge, home. He is protected with equipment and wears his cap backward. He is always right-handed. He is the most Yin of the defensive players. He is indirectly involved in every play. He is the mother, the healer, the nurturer, the receiver, guiding the father in his decisions, consoling him for his mistakes. Balanced, he is flexible to many pitchers, dependable, obedient, and quick to act. Imbalanced, he is slow, unsure, and inconstant. Physically he is big, powerful, and lumbering, possessing a strong arm. He is usually older, experienced, and wise. He is the belly of the defense.

☳ THE FIRST BASEMAN, CHEN, the Arouser

He is the first son and guards the first refuge, first base. Large, powerful, and steady, he arouses by his consistency with his glove and his bat. Defensively, he is indirectly involved in most putouts and resembles the catcher in his receptivity. Directly involved defensively, he initiates difficult plays with his intelligence and quickness of decision. He is often the father or leader of the next generation, that of the offense. He is usually the oldest of the infielders and left-handed for playing the Yin side of the infield. He is the feet of the defense.

━ ━ THE SECOND BASEMAN, K'AN,
━━━
━ ━ the Engulfer

He is the second son and guards the right side of the second refuge, second base. In the model of the ideal, the second baseman would play behind the pitcher and cover the gaps between second and both first and third. Since he has been reduced to a lesser role by the shortstop, his attributes of K'an have also been reduced. He nevertheless possesses the qualities of water and is dangerous to the opposition. In character, he is closer to the pitcher than the catcher, and his speed and fluidity are essential for his position. He is smaller, quicker, and younger. He is less developed defensively than the shortstop, playing the Yin side of the infield. Imbalanced, he is impatient and temperamental. Balanced, he is calm and far-reaching. He is the left ear of the defense.

THE THIRD BASEMAN, KEN,
the Silencer

He is the third son and guards the second-to-last refuge, third base. The third baseman is similar to the first baseman in character. He is powerful and strong but younger and more agile than the first son. Possessing a strong arm and bat, he is usually soft-spoken and modest. He is always right-handed for playing the Yang side of the infield. He is usually not as established a hitter as the first baseman. Advancing age often leads him to first base. When called upon defensively, he is solid and impenetrable. Balanced, he possesses the qualities of the rock (mountain). He is the hands of the defense.

THE SHORTSTOP, K'AN,
the Engulfer

He is the twin second son and guards the left side of the second refuge, second base. The shortstop is the dominant twin of the second baseman. The two possess the greatest instinct for one another, second only in relation to the pitcher and the catcher. His attributes are identical to the second baseman's: smaller, quicker, and younger. He is usually more developed than his twin for playing the Yang side of second base. His direct involvement defensively is second only to the pitcher's. Balanced, he is flowing, graceful, and calm; imbalanced, he is emotional and inconsistent, often succeeding in the difficult while failing in the routine. Balanced offensively, he is a more powerful hitter than his twin; imbalanced, he is second only to the pitcher in futility. He is the right ear of the defense.

The Outfielders

The outfielders play a less active role in the defense than the infielders. They are more Yin than the infield, and the infield is more Yang than the outfield. Their role defensively is often one of routine, but when called upon, their plays can become ones of extremes, covering the most ground, requiring the longest throws, and demanding the most adventurous catches. For these reasons I have indicated them as the three daughters of the family.

THE LEFT FIELDER, SUN, the Penetrator

He is like the first daughter and guards the Yin side of the outfield. The left fielder is usually more gifted with his bat than with his glove or arm. He is strong, slower, and powerful, although not as balanced as the center fielder. He is often either slower and a power hitter, or extremely fast and a contact hitter. He is usually the eldest of the outfielders. He resembles his brother, the first baseman, and like the first baseman, the position is often the final defensive role of older players. Balanced, he is fleet, penetrating the difficult; imbalanced, he is a liability on the field. He is indicated as wind and wood (lumber) and is the thighs of the defense.

THE CENTER FIELDER, LI, the Illuminator

He is like the second daughter and covers the heart of the outfield. The center fielder is usually the most balanced player on the team, having a good arm, glove, and bat. He is stronger and faster than his opposite twins, the second baseman and shortstop. With his speed and prowess in the outfield and on the base paths, he is often the leader of the team, lighting the way when he is the leadoff or power hitter. Balanced, he is the complete player; imbalanced, he is inconsistent with his glove and arm or an offensive liability. He is fire, the eyes of the defense.

THE RIGHT FIELDER, TUI, the Uplifter

He is like the third daughter and guards the Yang side of the outfield. The right fielder is often second only to the center fielder in balance. He is usually more gifted with the bat and slower in the field than the center fielder. He is often the power hitter of the team. He is the mirror of his brother, the third baseman, and possesses an equally strong arm. Balanced, he uplifts the team with his confidence in winning and demonstration of timely hits and assists to third base and to the plate. Imbalanced, he lacks confidence and is inconsistent. He is the lake and the marsh, the mouth of the defense.

THE TAO OF PITCHING

There is the Yang of right-handed pitchers;
There is the Yin of left-handed pitchers.
That which is seen every day becomes the familiar and Yang, while that which is occasionally seen becomes the unfamiliar and Yin. This is like writing with the opposite hand. Reversing the habitual, we have to begin all over again.
There is the Yang of the starter;
There is the Yin of the closer.
Long work requires rhythm and endurance and is Yang, while short work requires adaptability and intensity and is Yin. Entering in the beginning, one has time to remedy one's mistakes; entering in the end, one has no room to err.
There is the Yang of power pitchers;
There is the Yin of off-speed pitchers.
Challenging Yang with Yang, nothing is left to speculation.
Challenging Yang with Yin and Yin with Yang, everything is left to speculation.
There is the Yang of young arms;
There is the Yin of old arms.

Youth makes up for inexperience with energy;
Old age makes up for energy with experience.
Longevity depends upon fluidity;
Transience depends upon inflexibility.
There is the Yang of pitching;
There is the Yin of fielding.
Focusing only on Yang, one is surprised by Yin;
Focusing only on Yin, one neglects Yang.
After the pitch, the pitcher becomes a fielder;
With runners on base, the fielder becomes a pitcher.
Completing one action at a time develops right intent;
Starting one action before completing another develops wrong in-
    tent.
Intent on holding the runner, the pitcher walks the next batter;
Intent on the strike out, he misplays the comebacker to the mound.
There is the Yang of the ball;
There is the Yin of the air.
There is the Yang of the arm;
There is the Yin of the wrist and fingers.
Yang relies on the arm propelling the ball as fast as possible;
Yin relies on the wrist and fingers, rotating the seams and moving
    the ball through the air.

As can be seen, pitching conforms to the laws of the Tao.

As a young player grows, his Yang is increasing. His best pitch is his fastball, which he occasionally mixes with inconsistent breaking and off-speed pitches. The greater his velocity, the less his control. This kind of inexperienced pitcher is referred to as a thrower. His raw talent will often give him the opportunity to start or relieve in games.

Coaches, who have seen it all more than once, will prepare this prospect for the reality of what is to come. Control and off-speed pitches must be developed if his career is to have any duration.

Yang is complemented by Yin. A hitter will eventually adjust to the consistency of Yang (unless the pitcher possesses incredible Yang). Mixing Yang with Yin creates an imbalance for the hitter. Diminishing Yang is augmented with Yin. The strength and resiliency of youth can never be regained; Yang cannot be replenished with Yang. Yin must be patiently cultivated to the point where a pitcher has the confidence to use it in difficult situations. Youth is afraid of yielding to Yin only because it is new. Reassurance leads to belief; belief leads to success; success leads to independence; independence leads to reassurance.

On the other hand, there are young, disciplined pitchers who, lacking the unbridled Yang of the power pitcher, have developed several pitches. When a pitcher can shift location, mix speeds, and use a variety of pitches, the hitter begins to think—and thinking at the plate is the greatest enemy of the hitter. Thinking Yin, he is given Yang. Even the average fastball of an off-speed pitcher looks deceptively fast when it is unexpected. An off-speed and control pitcher is a more balanced pitcher, augmenting his modest skills through practice and knowledge of the hitters. Enhancing Yin with Yang and Yang with Yin, he is difficult to solve and unpredictable. A Yin pitcher will expend less energy and will have a longer career than a Yang pitcher.

A fastball pitcher whose every pitch is the same, and whose only consideration is whether any hitter can catch up to his fastball, is an example of extreme Yang. There is also his complement, a pitcher of extreme Yin, whose every pitch is the same and whose only consideration is whether any hitter can wait long enough for the ball. He is the knuckleballer.

This is the greatest Yin a pitcher can develop. The pitcher, by throwing the ball with only the slightest rotation, yields the ball completely to the mercy of the wind and air. Since no man can know the intent of the wind, the ball moves like a leaf; not even the pitcher knows where it will end up. By yielding Yang for Yin, the knuckleball pitcher conserves energy. Yang becomes an enemy for Yin; throwing the ball too hard or with too much spin will diminish its effect. The knuckleballer is the final expression of the secret of endurance. Even though the knuckleball is the most difficult pitch to throw, if the pitcher has mastered his art, he will invariably pitch into his forties. He is also rare, as so few believe in yielding. After a lifetime of resisting diminishing Yang, it is hard to submit to increasing Yin. If only we knew.

Finally, there is the Tao or complete pitcher. When Yin and Yang are balanced, there is nothing a pitcher cannot do. He has every skill he needs. He is gifted because he has unceasingly worked to be gifted. He commands the moment, the opposition, the game, and himself. While he is on the mound, the world is his. His only weaknesses are time and injury.

The secret of pitching is simple:

Pitch one pitch at a time.

Make every pitch count.

Take advantage of your defense. A strike out takes a minimum of
    three pitches; a groundout but one.

Take advantage of your mistakes.

Changing Yin into Yang,

You must not be afraid to create good from bad.

Putting runners on base, you induce the force-out and double play;

falling behind in the count, you come back with your best pitch.
Pitch from your center.
Throwing from your legs, your pitches are wild;
Throwing from your arm, you force your strength and injure your-
self;
Throwing from your hand, your pitches flatten out;
Throwing from your head, you aim and miss your location.
Pitching from your center, the body and mind unite.
The center instinctively commands the head, the head the legs, the
legs the arm, the arm the hand, the hand the ball, and the ball
commands the spirit of your center.

The center is the point of balance, the place of harmony, the sea of Tao. Only when the mind is empty and clearly focused can you pitch from your center. When you think, the hitter can read your thoughts. When you abandon yourself to the Tao, no man can read your spirit. You must *will* the ball to the location. Even though it has left your hand, it will continue to be directed and will miraculously find the mark every time, in the manner commanded.

This is the secret of pitching.

THE TAO OF OFFENSE

This batting order closely follows the established pattern of managers, starting with Yang (fastest runners and strongest hitters) and ending with Yin (slowest runners and weakest hitters).

The trigrams roughly correspond to a player's defensive trigram, with one glaring exception: the pitcher. Traditionally, the best hitter bats in the fourth or cleanup position, and this is indicated as ☰ , the creator. No modern-day pitcher bats fourth, however. He is the opposite, ☷ , the receiver, and bats in the last position, in a role of sacrificing. This indicates an imbalance.

When young boys first begin to play baseball, it is common that the best thrower is also the best hitter. This rarely happens in the majors. Pitching has become a specialized position in the modern era, to the degree that we have taken the bat completely out of the pitcher's hands and put it into the hands of the designated hitter.

It is true that pitching is the most demanding of any position, followed by catching, and that the strain put on a starting pitcher's arm only allows him to pitch every four to five days. And good pitchers have become a commodity that many managers would rather not risk at the plate. How then can he be as accomplished a hitter as an everyday player? Nevertheless, if practice was encouraged on a continuous basis and the designated hitter abolished, pitchers, with their natural ability for baseball, could also prove to be reliable hitters.

Some might feel that the father $\equiv$, being the leader of the family, should lead off in the number one position. In exceptional cases, this could be true, but in the day-to-day routine, it is more natural to let the younger members of the family start the business at hand and have the father enter at the time of greatest responsibility.

It might prove advantageous in a pennant playoff or World Series to start the best hitter first or second. He is the leader offensively, and continuing to rely on patterns that worked over 162 games will not always work in a 7-game series. Perhaps this could be one remedy for the slumps often associated with postseason play.

This batting order follows the most common orders. In reality, it will vary depending upon the ability, age, and talent of the team, and individual managing philosophies. A more balanced order could be achieved by spreading the wealth around. Instead of starting off with extreme Yang, and then tapering to extreme Yin, it would be divided into three divisions of Yang/Yin/Yang (speed, sacrifice, and power).

The Batting Order

1 ⚊⚊ LI, Lightning (Fire), the Second Daughter

The player who starts off the inning sets the spirit for the offense. His intent is to get on base. He is a contact hitter, seldom striking out and patient at the plate, who knows a walk is as good as a base hit. Preferably, he is a switch hitter. Once on first, he is a threat to steal second and third and thereby disrupt the pitcher's concentration. He is the best base runner and leads the team in stolen bases. He is usually the center fielder ☵ , or his mirrors, the second baseman ☵ , or shortstop ☵ . Occasionally, he is the left fielder ☵ .

Lightning strikes to illuminate the way.

2 ☵ K'AN, the Twin Engulfer, the Second Son, Rain (Water)

The second hitter is a good contact hitter, hitting to all fields and seldom striking out. His intent is to advance the first runner when he is on base or—should the first hitter fail to get on—to assume the role of leadoff hitter. He should therefore be a fast base runner and preferably a left-handed or switch hitter. Should both runners get on base, they become an early threat and distract the pitcher. The second hitter is usually the second baseman ☵ , left fielder ☵ , or occasionally the third baseman ☵ .

After lightning comes the rain.

3 ☳ CHEN, the Arouser, the First Son, Thunder

The third hitter is the second-best hitter on the team and perhaps the best overall hitter. His intent is to score or advance the lead runners. He is a power hitter, capable of hitting to all fields. He often bats left-handed, to pull the ball through the gap created by holding the runner on at first base. He is usually the first baseman ☵ , or his mirror, the left fielder ☳ , and occasionally the right fielder ☶ or center fielder ☲ .

When the rains clear, the thunder rumbles.

4 ☰ CHIEN, the Creator, the Father, Heaven

The cleanup hitter is the best hitter on the team. A team's offensive strength can be measured by this player. His intent is to score runners. He concentrates on making contact and not on home runs; his natural skill will account for the long ball. Ideally, he is fast, should he lead off an inning. He should have few weaknesses, hitting both left- and right-handed pitchers with authority. He is patient at the plate as pitchers are deliberately cautious with him.

He is usually the first baseman ☷ , the left fielder ☳ , or right fielder ☶ . Occasionally he is the center fielder ☲ , and rarer the catcher ☵ , or shortstop ䷜ .

Thunder clears the way for heaven.

5 ☴ SUN, the Penetrator, the First Daughter, the Wind

The fifth position is usually occupied by the third-best hitter on the team, but he is often not as disciplined and is more prone to strike out than the third and fourth hitters. He often leads the team in home runs, but has a lower batting average and RBI total. The stronger the hitter in this position is, the more dangerous the fourth hitter becomes, since the opposition cannot afford to pitch around him. This fifth hitter is usually the left fielder ☳ , or his mirror, the right fielder ☶ , or the third baseman ☷ . Occasionally he is the catcher ☵ .

Heaven comes round through the wind.

6 ═══ KEN, the Silencer, the Third Son, the Mountain

Power is advantageous in the sixth position, since this hitter often comes to the plate with runners on base. A good spot for developing hitters. Modesty and discipline are the keys. He is usually the third baseman ═══ , or his mirror, the right fielder ═══ . Occasionally he is the catcher ═══ .

The winds clear the mists to reveal the mountain.

7 ═══ TUI, the Uplifter, the Third Daughter, the Lake

Speed is an asset in the seventh position. Should the first six hitters be retired in order, he becomes the leadoff man in the third inning. He possesses the attributes of the leadoff hitter but to a lesser degree. He is often a better fielder than hitter, but shows some offensive potential. He is usually the right fielder ═══ or his mirror, the third baseman ═══ . Occasionally he is the shortstop ═══ or his twin.

At the bottom of the mountain stands the lake.

8 ─x─ ─o─ ─x─ K'AN, the Twin Engulfer, the Twin Second Son, the Rain

Any offense contributed from this position is an advantage. It is usually delegated to strong defensive players. A disciplined hitter can produce some RBIs from this spot. He will sacrifice runners if the pitcher who follows is to be replaced by a pinch hitter. He is usually the shortstop ☵ , or his twin, the second baseman ☳ , or catcher ☷ .

The lake draws upward to rain.

9 ── ── ── K'UN, the Receiver, the Mother, the Earth

The reason for the designated hitter. The ninth spot is strictly reserved for the pitcher. With runners on, skill in bunting is essential. A pitcher who comes to the plate with confidence can often surprise the opposing pitcher who has let down his guard. He will occasionally win games as a pitcher because of his success at the plate. Even the worst-hitting pitcher is better than the designated hitter.

The rain brings forth life from the earth.

THE TAO OF
HITTING

There is the Yang of right-handed hitters;
There is the Yin of left-handed hitters;
There is the Tao of the switch-hitter.
There is the Yang of the home run;
There is the Yin of the bunt.
There is the Yang of hitting for power;
There is the Yin of hitting for average.
There is the Tao of the complete hitter.
There is the Yang of pulling the ball;
There is the Yin of hitting to the opposite field.
There is the Tao of going with the pitch.
There is the Yang of the center of the bat;
There is the Yin of the handle and the end of the bat.
There is the Tao of the bat.
There is the Yang of hitting with runners on base;
There is the Yin of hitting with nobody on.
There is the Yang of advancing the runners with hits;

There is the Yin of advancing the runners with sacrifices.
There is the Tao of the situation hitter.

Go to the plate with conviction, believing you will hit the ball during every at bat; if you possess doubts, you will certainly fail. Your belief must be complete; talking to yourself won't work, because this involves thinking, and thinking is just too slow. When you can focus all of your energy, your conviction will be strong; when you cannot focus all of your energy, your conviction will be weak. You must therefore come to the plate full of conviction and empty of any thought.

Wait for the ball, it will come to you. When you see the ball clearly, you will be able to hit it. Your eyes will guide your bat. Go with the pitch; the pitch will never go with you. In this way, the situation will dictate the hit. A pitcher will exploit your weaknesses; if you have no weaknesses, you will exploit the pitcher.

Focus on everything; concentrate on nothing. The pitcher, the pitch, the count, the situation, the way you feel, the bat in your hands, all must become one single feeling. In this way you will understand the flow between everything and know the intent as it unfolds.

The Tao of Good Timing

There are no secrets to hitting the ball;
There are many secrets to missing the ball.
Timing is simple, cultivating it is difficult.
Hard work develops discipline;
Discipline develops intent;
Intent develops patience;
Patience develops faith.
Therefore,
Trying to hit without hard work, you lack skill.
Trying to hit without discipline, you lack consistency.
Trying to hit without intent, you lack focus.
Trying to hit without patience, you lack timing.
Trying to hit without faith, you lack energy.
Likewise,
Skill develops consistency,
Consistency develops focus,
Focus develops timing,
Timing develops energy.
This is the essence of good timing.

The Tao of the Strike Zone

Always attempt to hit the ball with the center of the bat.

Pitches on the outside of the strike zone are Yin;

Pitches in the center of the strike zone are Yang.

Pitches on the inside (Yin) must be swung on early to hit them with the center (Yang) of the bat to pull the ball.

Pitches on the outside (Yin) must be swung on late to hit them with the center (Yang) of the bat to drive the ball to the opposite field.

Pitches down the center (Yang) must be swung on perfectly to hit them with the center (Yin) of the bat to power the ball to all fields.

This is why the balls you hit the farthest feel effortless.

Therefore,

A hitter must be faster on inside pitches.

A hitter must be slower on outside pitches.

A hitter must be just right on pitches down the middle.

When pitched inside, a hitter with insufficient Yang will be jammed.

When pitched outside, a hitter with insufficient Yang will have no power.

When pitched down the center, a hitter with insufficient Yin will make pop-ups and fly balls.

Willing and Wanting the Hit

Will the hit; never want the hit.

Wanting to make contact, you wait for your pitch and miss opportunities.

Willing to make contact, you wait for no pitch and take advantage of opportunities.

Wanting to hit home runs, you strike out often.

Willing to just hit the ball, you hit your share of home runs, triples, doubles, and singles.

Wanting the right pitch, you swing at bad pitches and take good
 pitches.
Willing for the right pitch, you lay off of bad pitches and hit good
 pitches.
Wanting to hit it where they ain't, you hit it where they are.
Willing to hit it where they ain't, you hit it where they ain't.
Wanting to sacrifice, you fail to execute.
Willing to sacrifice, you move the runner over.

Therefore,
Make a habit of having no habit.
Make a ritual of having no ritual.
Make a desire of having no desire.
Make a thought of having no thought.

Everything else will follow in its place.

THE TAO OF THE
OBJECTIVES

Or One Man's Yang is
Another Man's Yin

Having the baseball, the field, the players, and the rules as the shared common elements, the game can now begin.

The objective of both teams is to win.

The objective of the offense is to score runs; the objective of the defense is to prevent runs.

The objective of the pitcher is to prevent the batter from reaching base. His ideal objective is to pitch a no-hitter, or ultimately a perfect game. This would be extreme Yang for the defense and extreme Yin for the opposing offense.

The objective of the hitter is to advance around all four bases. His ideal objective is to hit a home run, or ultimately a grand slam. This would be extreme Yang for the offense and extreme Yin for the opposing defense.

The objective of the fielders is to prevent the batter from advancing around all four bases. Their ideal objective is an out at the plate, or ultimately a triple play. This would be extreme Yang for the defense and extreme Yin for the opposing offense.

The hitter attempts to hit the ball as far away from home plate as possible, with the exception of the bunt, to create time to advance around as many bases as he can, thereby creating time for any other base runners to complete their cycle.

The defense attempts to keep the ball as close to home plate as possible, to erase the time the runner has to advance around the bases.

The offense completes the cycle in a counterclockwise motion, always advancing the runner closest to completion.

The defense arrests the cycle in a clockwise motion, always trying to erase the runner closest to completion.

Therefore:

The farther the ball touches the ground from home plate, the greater the Yang for the offense and the greater the Yin for the defense.

The closer the ball is to home plate, the greater the Yin for the offense and the greater the Yang for the defense.

The farther a runner advances around the bases, the greater the Yang for the offense and the greater the Yin for the defense.

From the Perspective of the Offense

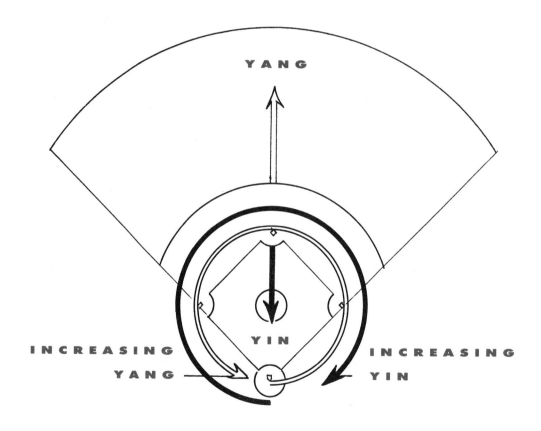

The closer the runner remains to home plate, the greater the Yin for the offense and the greater the Yang for the defense.

From the Perspective of the Defense

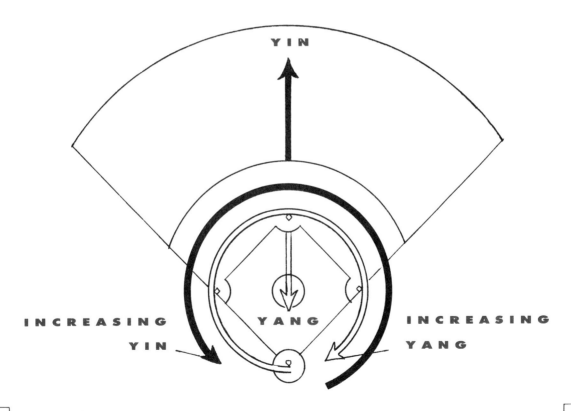

YIN

INCREASING YIN   YANG   INCREASING YANG

FROM THE OBJECTIVE TO THE DETERMINED

Yin and Yang can be seen from a common perspective of the Objective and the Determined. The Objective and the Determined are completed expressions of the Tao. They exist before the game (the Objective) and after the game (the Determined). Thus, both teams set out with the shared Objective of winning the game by scoring more runs than the other during nine innings of play, and whoever Determines this Objective is declared the winner.

Both teams take to the field on an equal or neutral basis. As soon as the first pitch is thrown, however, everything starts to be Determined in expressions of Yin and Yang. From the moment the umpire calls "Play ball," the game is in progress.

A ball "in play" or "in flight," or a play "in jeopardy," is neither Yin nor Yang. It is pure Tao, awaiting resolution, awaiting expression, awaiting the unknown. The play is timeless, but it will be determined by time. It is this element of the unknown that gives the game its suspense. It is the suspended moment in time that gives the game its sense of awe.

Both the Objective and the Determined are completed expressions of the Tao. What is Yang for the offense is Yin for the defense; what is Yin for the offense is Yang for the defense—but only one team can walk off the field a victor.

THE TAO OF
PERSPECTIVE

From the Perspective of the Offense	**From the Perspective of the Defense**
There is the Yang of safe; There is the Yin of out.	There is the Yang of out; There is the Yin of safe.
There is the Yang of balls; There is the Yin of strikes.	There is the Yang of strikes; There is the Yin of balls.
There is the Yang of bases on balls; There is the Yin of called out on strikes.	There is the Yang of called out on strikes; There is the Yin of bases on balls.
There is the Yang of hitting safely; There is the Yin of putouts.	There is the Yang of putouts; There is the Yin of hitting safely.

There is the Yang of home
runs;
There is the Yin of strike outs.

There is the Yang of runs
batted in;
There is the Yin of men left on
base.

There is the Yang of the bases
loaded;
There is the Yin of nobody on.

There is the Yang of sending
the runner;
There is the Yin of double
plays.

There is the Yang of extra
bases;
There is the Yin of outs
advancing.

There is the Yang of strike
outs;
There is the Yin of home runs.

There is the Yang of men left
on base;
There is the Yin of runs batted
in.

There is the Yang of nobody
on;
There is the Yin of the bases
loaded.

There is the Yang of double
plays;
There is the Yin of sending
the runner.

There is the Yang of outs
advancing;
There is the Yin of extra
bases.

There is the Yang of line
  drives;
There is the Yin of pop-ups.
There is the Yang of errors;
There is the Yin of robbing
  hits.

There is the Yang of sacrifices;
There is the Yin of stranding
  the runner.

There is the Yang of stolen
  bases;
There is the Yin of caught
  stealing.

There is the Yang of pop-ups;
There is the Yin of line drives.

There is the Yang of robbing
  hits;
There is the Yin of errors.

There is the Yang of stranding
  the runner;
There is the Yin of sacrifices.

There is the Yang of caught
  stealing;
There is the Yin of stolen
  bases.

THE TAO OF
KEEPING
SCORE

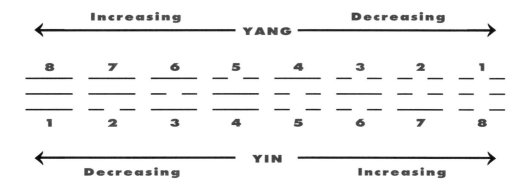

Upon further examination, the Ancients realized the world was more complicated than Three and the Eight Trigrams, and they proceeded to combine the trigrams into pairs forming Sixty-four Hexagrams.

Now it has come to me, from the groundwork of the Ancients, that the laws of baseball cannot be completely represented by the duality of Yin and Yang. It cannot be encompassed by the trigrams completely because baseball was not directly modeled after the science of the Tao.

In baseball, advancement (Yang) is expressed in Fours:

4 balls = 1 walk
4 bases = 1 run
4 wins = 1 World Series ring

Arrestment (Yin) is expressed in Threes:

3 strikes = 1 out
3 outs   = 1 side retired

Yang can now be expressed in four increasing degrees of Yang; Yin can now be expressed in three increasing degrees of Yin. And because Yang and Yin are competing with each other for completion, the two can be expressed together. Whichever is completed first is considered the victor.

Yang and Yin Model for Representing Strikes and Balls

YIN
Increasing (cannot decrease)

YANG ⟶ **YIN** **(Completion)**

STRIKES

— — — — —
— — — — —
— — — — —

0   1   2   3 (Out)

YANG
Increasing (cannot decrease)

YIN ⟶ **YANG** **(Completion)**

BALLS

— — — — —
— — — — —
— — — — —
— — — — —

0   1   2   3   4 (Walk)

Representing the Count

Since balls and strikes oppose each other, the count can be expressed as strikes over balls:

Strikes
——— ——— — — — —
——— ——— — — — —
——— ——— — — — —

Maximum Yin Completion (Strike out with no balls)

Balls
— — — — — — — —
— — — — — — — —
— — — — — — — —

Count (Balls/Strikes)   0/0   0/1   0/2   0/3

Strikes
———— ———— ———— ———— ————
———— ———— ———— ———— ————
———— ———— ———— ———— ————

Maximum Yang Completion (Walk on 4 pitches)

Balls
— — — — — — — —— ————
— — — — — — — —— ————
— — — — — — — —— ————

Count (Balls/Strikes)   0/0   1/0   2/0   3/0   4/0

Strikes							

Balls							
Count	0/0	0/1	1/1	1/2	2/2	3/2	3/3
(Balls/Strikes)						Full Count	Strike Out

Yin and Yang cannot occur at the same time; a pitch is either a strike or a ball (a hitter can swing at a ball, but this makes it a strike.)

Yin and Yang cannot complete at the same time; the result of a time at bat is either a strike out or a walk. This is the law of Either/Or.

A full count is the deciding or breaking point for completion. Yin completing before Yang is a strike out, Yang completing before Yin is a walk.

This is a pure model for the count. A player can interrupt the count at any time by hitting the ball fair. This outcome requires another model identical to the count model.

Representing Hits and Outs

Hits can be expressed as four increasing degrees of Yang in tetragrams.

YIN ⟶ YANG

HITS

| At Bat | Single | Double | Triple | Home Run | Yang complete |

To score a run, a player must cross all four bases before three men are put out.

Outs can be represented as three increasing degrees of Yin in a trigram.

YANG ⟶ YIN

OUTS

| 0 | 1 | 2 | 3 | Yin Completion Side Retired |

Representing Runners on Base

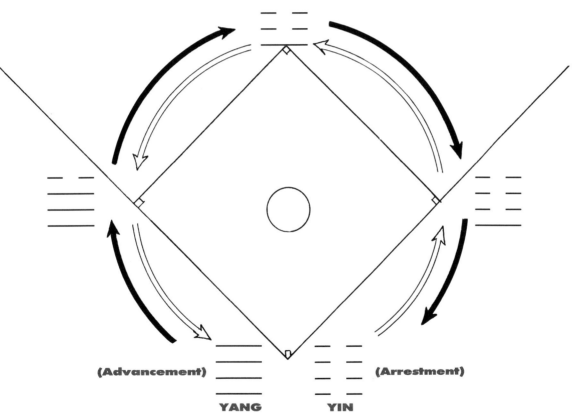

The Field of Play

(Advancement)

(Arrestment)

YANG

YIN

To score a run, all four bases must be crossed.

A player's advancement around the bases can be represented in four increasing degrees of Yang in a tetragram.

YIN ⟶ YANG

Bases					**Yang Completion**
Runner On	**At Bat**	**1st**	**2nd**	**3rd**	**Home (Run Scores)**

To represent base runners, we are faced with a choice since more than one runner can be on base. If each runner's advancement is represented separately, as on a scoring card, then the model is identical to the hit model. If each runner's advancement is represented collectively, then the model could either look like this

YIN ⟶ YANG

Nobody On	**1st**	**2nd**	**1st & 2nd**	**3rd**	**1st & 3rd**	**Bases Loaded**	**Run Scores (Still Loaded)**

with broken or Yin lines representing unoccupied bases, or the model could look like this

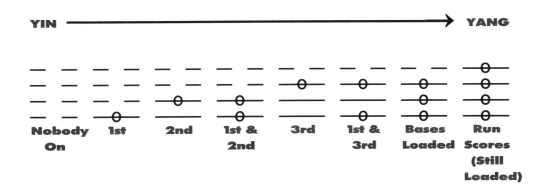

with a solid line with a circle representing the runner.

All of this is not to suggest an alternative way of scoring a game (although it could be used in this way), but it is only to show how the Tao is at work resolving itself in terms of Yin and Yang.

When the situation is one of active Yang and dormant Yin, the offense is in control of the game, or is influencing the Tao. For example, if the bases were loaded with none out and a count of three balls and no strikes to the batter, the situation would be represented as:

Count
———
Strikes ——— Outs ———
———
0   0

— —   — —
———   ———
Balls ———   Runners   ———
———   On   ———
———   ———
3   Bases
Loaded

In this situation a home run would be

———
———
———
———

This is the maximum resolve of Yang. From here Yang would return to Yin, with a new batter (and likely a new pitcher), a new count, no men on base, with still none out, however.

Conversely, when the situation is one of active Yin and dormant Yang, the defense is in control of the game, or is influencing the Tao. For example, if none were on with two out and a count of two

strikes and no balls to the batter, the situation would be represented as:

Count

Strikes	— —	
	— —	
	2	

Outs	— —	
	— —	
	2	

	— —	
Balls	— —	
	— —	
	0	

	— —	
Runners On	— —	
	— —	
	0	

**In this situation a strike out
would be**

— —
— —
— —

This would be the maximum resolve of Yin. From there, Yin would
return to Yang. The defense, having retired the side in order, would
come to the plate as offense.

These types of plays are considered exciting because they mani-
fest extremes of either Yin or Yang. Its beauty and strength lie in
the total domination of one opponent over the other. This is also

its weakness, because a one-sided match lacks tension and can quickly become boring if the one-sidedness continues. Tension and the essence of the game arise when both Yin and Yang approach their climaxes or points of completion at the same time. For example, the bases loaded, two out, the count full, in the bottom of the ninth inning, with the home team down by one run in the seventh game of the World Series.

	Count				**Wins**	**Losses**
Strikes	— —	**Outs**	— —		— —	— —
	— —		— —			
	2		**2**			
					3	**3**
	— —	**Runners**	— —			
Balls		**On**				
	— —		— —			
	3	**Bases Loaded**				

The entire year has come down to one pitch for resolution. A single scoring two runs would end the game—and Yang would complete itself before Yin. A third strike will also end the game—with Yin completing itself before Yang. Resolution will always be expressed with either a completed Yang and an incompleted Yin or a completed Yin and an incompleted Yang.

THE TAO OF
SAFE AND OUT

or Life and Death on the Diamond

Safe is Yang and life.

Out is Yin and death.

The Tao is thus expressed in completion, as it is in life. A circle completed from beginning to end without interruption constitutes a run or advancement, as an action in life completed from beginning to end without interruption or death constitutes an advancement. Nothing tangible has been accomplished, but we have somehow made progress toward an understanding.

The counterclockwise completion of the circle is a rare example of baseball's going against the natural laws of the Tao. A clockwise completion would have made the game more harmonious, but if you start off backward you have to finish backward. The circle of life usually runs in a clockwise motion:

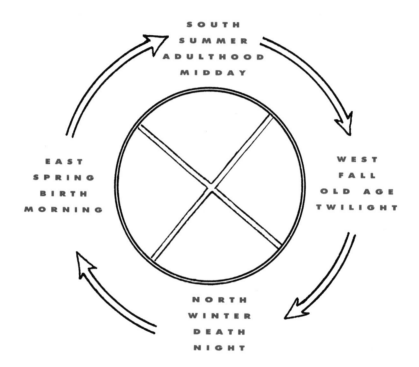

SOUTH
SUMMER
ADULTHOOD
MIDDAY

EAST
SPRING
BIRTH
MORNING

WEST
FALL
OLD AGE
TWILIGHT

NORTH
WINTER
DEATH
NIGHT

A ball hit into the ever-expanding field of the Tao must be sent back in to the finite source before the player who sent it out has time to complete the cycle. When the runner crosses home plate before the ball, Yang eclipses Yin and he is alive.

When the ball crosses home plate before the runner, then Yin eclipses Yang and he is dead.

This is a higher level of the Tao of baseball, the runner becoming Yang and the ball his life span or Tao. The ball holds both the potential for life and death. Thrown toward the strike zone or the hitter's heart, he must protect the plate or his life, creating an opportunity to make something of his life. A pop-up is only an illusion of accomplishment, for although the runner has the time to touch the bases, unless the ball hits the ground, his progress is in vain. When he successfully hits the ball, he ventures into the unknown, the bases becoming islands of Yang in a sea of Yin. As the ball travels away from him, it becomes Yang and he advances; as the ball travels back toward him, it becomes Yin and death, and he must find refuge on the nearest base. Should the ball arrive before him, or should he be caught in between bases, Yin arrests Yang and he is out and dead. Should he arrive before the ball, Yang eclipses Yin and he is still alive. Now he must either create more time by stealing a base or rely on his team to bring him home. Only when he crosses home plate before the ball or three outs has Yang truly eclipsed Yin and has his journey and life been completed without having tasted death.

The individual player's life and death leads to the collective team's life and death. Three outs and the team is retired; a run, and the entire team has scored. As the team lives, so do all of its players; and as the team dies, so do all of its players, regardless of their individual accomplishments.

Baseball can only be played one game at a time, and a team can only win or lose one game at a time. This is the Tao of daily life.

As the season progresses, wins and losses accumulate, and this becomes a higher measure of winning, that of attaining first place, of the collective eclipsing the individual. This is the Tao of the season.

From here, winning and losing enter into a different realm, that of the pennant. It begins a new, second season, everything else becoming history. This is the Tao of adulthood.

And from here, winning and losing enter into the final realm, that of the World Series. Everything that has gone before has led to one final game, one final out, one final victor, one final loser. This is the Tao of life and death.

Winning the World Series thus becomes an expression of extreme Yang, and losing of extreme Yin.

When viewed from another level, we can witness the Tao of baseball that contains no victor, no defeated. Here everything is predetermined and in harmony. Time is suspended and playing the game is the only thing that counts. It is better to have played every day for a last-place team than to have sat on the bench of a championship team.

Winning is Yang and losing is Yin only when winning is the only objective of playing baseball. As has often been pointed out, professional baseball is made up of grown men playing a child's game. This leads to a different perspective, for men will only play a child's game so long as they don't have to play a man's game.

We have all witnessed the intrusion of real life into the game: war, death, retirement, the weather, personal problems, and the ubiquitous injuries. A player whose life is disrupted by such an occurrence will tell you that winning and losing are secondary to having played the game—or to living life. In other words, the Tao has changed the Yang of winning into Yin in favor of the Yang of having graced the field.

THE TAO OF COMPLETION

Now the game takes time for Yin and Yang to complete themselves, but completion takes no time at all. The moment the final out is made or the winning run crosses the plate, the game is over. Bang! All that remains are memories of the events that determined the outcome or the completion of Yin or Yang. Winning and losing are not even short-lived; they are instantaneous! "It ain't over till it's over," but when it's over, it's over. Please consider this carefully.

Once Yin and Yang have been determined, they immediately return to their complement or opposite. When a game ends, another begins. When the season ends, another begins. Defense follows offense, offense follows defense. Wins follow losses, losses follow wins. This is why the Tao is represented as a circle, and why Yin and Yang are enclosed within the circle.

It is true that the offense can score indefinitely until the third out is made, but even then, each time the offense clears the bases, they are empty again.

This is not to say that Yin and Yang cannot complete themselves at the same time. We have become accustomed to looking for the duality of a winner and a loser and often forget other perspectives. Who really wins? Who gains more? Winning is intoxicating; losing is sobering. Winning is the pinacle, but leads to decline; losing is the lowest point, but leads to incline. The winner is self-satisfied; the loser is ambitious. The winner lives for yesterday; the loser for tomorrow. The winner is happy; the loser is sad. This is why winning and losing are best left to fate, and why players should concentrate on playing the game.

When Yin and Yang complete at the same time, however, there is total consumption, total satisfaction, total harmony, total joy, total peace. Does the sun compete with the moon for dominance of the earth? When a man and a woman create a child, do they not create and complete it at the same time? When we help those in need, is not everyone enriched? Or when we educate the ignorant, do we not both learn? Perhaps we focus too much on gain all the time and forget its complement, loss. There is nothing to fear in completion. It is through completion that we understand the whole.

T H E

COMMENTARIES

T H E
TAO OF
STRATEGY

Overcoming your opponent is simple:
When confronted with Yang, employ Yin;
When facing Yin, employ Yang.
Your success will depend upon your ability to discern the two.
Consider this carefully.

For example, when confronted with a fastball pitcher, which is Yang, employ Yin by taking pitches, working the count, bunting, choking up on the bat, sacrificing, and stealing and hitting and running late in counts. Try to force full-count situations. Disrupt a Yang pitcher's timing by making him throw over to first and second when runners are on base, and by making him throw as many pitches as possible. Always make him prove his control.

When confronted with an off-speed pitcher, which is Yin, employ Yang by swinging on the first pitch and early in counts, stealing and hitting and running early in the count, and by swinging for the fences. Never give a Yin pitcher time to use his stuff.

Likewise, when facing a power-hitting team, which is Yang, employ a Yin defense of starting an off-speed (preferably left-handed) pitcher, working the count, keeping the ball low and away, and slowing down the game. Intentionally walk batters in danger-ous situations, and play for the force-out and double-play ball.

When confronted with a fast, contact-hitting team, which is Yin, employ a Yang defense by starting a fastball (preferably right-handed) pitcher, throwing strikes, pitching high and inside, work-ing fast, and keeping men off the bases. Concentrate more on the hitters when there are men on base. In dangerous situations, go for the strike out or pop-up.

When your opponent's Yang approximates your Yang, be the first to
  act;
When your opponent's Yin approximates your Yin, be the last to act.
Never hesitate to be the first or the last.

For example, playing a Yang-against-Yang game, where either both pitchers are fireballers or both teams possess a power-hitting lineup, requires a very simple strategy: beat them fast and beat them early. Once a power pitcher finds his groove, he is difficult to upset. He is most vulnerable early. Likewise, a power-hitting team develops more confidence with each run scored. It is important to shut them down early and quickly, with one-two-three innings, and to avoid walks, which increase (their) chances of scoring big.

A Yin-against-Yin game, where either both starters are off-speed pitchers or both batting lineups possess contact hitters and fast runners, is much more of a challenge: strategically the best path is to outlast and outwit your opponent. This requires doing the unexpected. Bunt with two strikes, hit-and-run on the first pitch, throw breaking pitches on a full count, try double steals, suicide squeezes, switch-hitters, and use as many pitchers as necessary. One run is often the margin of victory in these types of games. It's important to play for that one run and defend against it. Play the infield in with a runner on third—unless there's also a runner on first with one out—and pitch out in potential hit-and-run and stealing situations. Instinct is the key.

Yin will overcome Yang if allowed the time to develop into Yang; Yang will overcome Yin if not allowed the time to develop into Yin.

For example, a Yin offense can overcome a Yang defense if they create enough time to allow themselves to develop into Yang. This means taking pitches, working the count, taking walks, stealing, sacrificing, hitting-and-running. Going down one-two-three on fewer than ten pitches is not going to win you anything in these types of games.

Likewise, a Yang defense must shut down a Yin offense—not giving them the time to develop into Yang—keeping them off the base paths by throwing strikes and by throwing hard and inside.

A Yang offense will overcome a Yin defense if it doesn't allow them enough time to develop into a Yang defense. This means swinging early, hitting-and-running, and swinging for the fences.

If you allow a Yin pitcher the time to use his full arsenal, you are your own worst enemy.

The Yang of Yang is power, confidence, and speed;
The Yin of Yang is fatigue, fear, and impatience.
The Yang of Yin is cunning, patience, and faith;
The Yin of Yin is chance, hesitation, and hope.

Play for as many runs as possible.
Finish the game as soon as possible.
Let your opponent beat you; never beat yourself.

Never give your opponent a second chance.
Let the situation dictate the action;
The game will always tell you what to do.
Remember, you overcome your opponent by being victorious within
yourself.

GŌ'S TWENTY-SIX RULES TO MANAGING YOUR WAY TO THE WORLD SERIES

1 *Place the team first.*
Being ruthless with the individual but devout to the whole,
Your players will learn the meaning of respect.

2 *Learn from your mistakes.*
There is no truer teacher than failure.
The right move is obvious after the wrong.
Why do you think they say "Most ball games are lost, not won"?

3 *Know yourself.*
By knowing yourself you will be able to know your players.
Turn on the light and people will stop fumbling in the dark.

4 *Be moderate from beginning to end.*
Building the fire too early, you run out of fuel;
Stoking it too late, you have too much left over.
What good is first place in June or second in October?

5 *Never antagonize your opponent.*
Arrogance rouses; humility lulls.
Is there any better advice than to let a sleeping dog lie?

6 *Manage your players; never let your players manage you.*
To build confidence, leave a player in; to teach discipline, take a
    player out.
Authority is obvious; so is negligence.

7 *Pay attention to details.*
Small things lead to big things.
If your players fail in the simple, how can they accomplish the
    great?

8 *Master fundamentals.*

What good is strategy if your team cannot execute it?

The stronger the fundamentals, the stronger the strategic potential.

9 *Treat all players the same.*

When confronted by twenty-four men, treat them as one; when confronted by one man, treat him as the twenty-four.

Biased, you separate; unbiased, you unite.

10 *Confide in no one.*

Consult as often as necessary, but decide alone.

By answering only to yourself,

You will be able to accept all criticism, offer no excuse, and take no credit.

11 *Manage for the team and not your critics.*

Catering to the front office, the press, and individual players, there is no end to your worries.

Satisfy the essential and you will silence the world.

Focus on what takes place between the white lines and everything outside of them will fall into place.

12 *Eschew anger in yourself and in your players.*
Presenting your case honorably to umpires, taking defeats in stride,
Your players will learn tolerance.

13 *Encourage, never discourage.*
Inferiority must be uprooted.
Superiority must be nurtured.

14 *Let the players play.*
A manager manages; a player plays.
There is no substitute for brilliance on the field.

15 *Avoid team rules.*
Broken rules must be punished; excessive behavior carries its own
   price.
If a player is doing his job, why interfere?
Solve problems before they arise.

16 *Use your entire roster.*
Relying only on your best is limiting.
Inexperience, given the chance, leads to experience.

17 *Look after your players' well-being.*
Nourish the spirit with spirit.
Nourish the body with exercise, rest, and proper food.

18 *Be resourceful.*
By looking to what you have rather than to what you don't,
You will turn loss into gain, weakness into strength.
The soft yields with the times; the hard breaks.

19 *Be judicious.*
Pardon the unavoidable, correct the avoidable.
When the body fails, it is destiny;
When the mind fails, who is to blame?

20 *Study the game and your opponents.*
By knowing the past you will understand the present.
By knowing your opponent you will understand yourself.
How can you play defense when you do not know your opponent's
    strength?
How can you play offense when you do not know his weakness?

21 *Never rely on the percentages.*
Let intuition be your guide.
Keeping your eyes only on the ground, you see the tracks and
 droppings but miss the game in the bush.
It is the real and not the unreal that is essential.

22 *Never hesitate.*
Runs cannot be taken off the scoreboard.
It is harder to score after missed opportunities.

23 *Create team spirit.*
Every player must feel a part, every player must contribute.
Winning is contagious; so is losing.

24 *Keep the game in perspective.*
Never sacrifice life for winning.
No one dies when you lose; no one goes to heaven when you win.

25 *Have faith.*
By believing in yourself, your players will believe in you.
By believing in your players, your players will believe in themselves.
By believing in the impossible, the impossible will be achieved.

26 *Manage by not managing.*
When the fans barely know your name,
When there is peace in the clubhouse,
When everyone is playing as a team,
When win follows win,
When the players believe they are doing it all themselves,
Then you are doing your job.

GŌ'S TWENTY RULES

FOR

PLAYER SUCCESS

1 *Do not be afraid of hard work.*
To last long, work long.
You do not make strong bones by making a show of muscles.

2 *Avoid superstition.*
Superstition is for those who do not know how.
When you know how, you can repeat at will.

3 *Accept defeat and victory equally.*
Never blame externals; never credit internals.
All victory and defeat come from the Tao.

4 *Seek out a good coach.*
Talent is inherent; proficiency is learned.
Two eyes are better than one.

5 *Do not become blinded by money.*
Focusing on the wealth of others will instill greed and jealousy
And distract you from the game.
Without the game, you wouldn't have a job.

6 *Remember your origins.*
A plant cannot grow without the earth.
In the same way, if you mistake yourself as your source,
You are rootless and destined to wither before fruition.

7 *Avoid alcohol, sex, and drugs.*
Depleting the life force, artificially replenishing the life force,
The body and spirit cannot rejuvenate. You will lose the essential
before your time.

8 *Do not make a show of religion.*
Be grateful in your heart and not on the microphone or in the
press.
Wear your cross where no man can see it.

9 *Give back to the game and the fan.*
Without the game, you could not realize your gift;
Without the fan, you could not realize your moment of glory.

10 *Restrain yourself.*
Rushing before you are ready, trying to prove yourself, you will fail.
Accepting your role, you will make the most of your chances.
Your game will convince others.

11 *Do not listen to the hype.*
Believing yourself to be immortal,
You leave yourself with no room to err.
When you do err, you will crumble like a city in an earthquake.
An earthquake gets a lot of hype.

12 *Never fear your opponent.*
Your opponent has the same objective as you.
If you see him otherwise, you create a dragon in the shape of a
    man.
Every man can be defeated.

13 *Intend your objective.*
The objective is attained through action.
Action is attained through intent.
Intending failure, you lose;
Intending success, you win.

14 *Simplify, never complicate.*
Hold something in the light and it becomes clear;
Put it in the dark and it becomes obscure.
The best method is always simple: keep your eye on the ball,
Take your cuts,
Throw strikes—home plate doesn't move.

15 *Open your mind.*
When you pitch, *see* the hitter.
When you hit, *see* the pitcher.
When you field, *see* the pitcher and hitter.
When you see yourself through the hitter, you will pitch.
When you see yourself through the pitcher, you will hit.
When you see yourself through the pitcher and hitter, you will field.

16 *Play with abandon and joy.*
If it's beyond your reach, you're not going to get it, so why worry.
If it's within your reach, you're going to get it, so why worry.
If you're not sure, you'd better dive for it; that way you won't have
   to worry.

17 *Cultivate patience.*
Impatient, you force the moment.
Overly patient, the moment passes you by.
What choice do you have but to know how to wait?

18 *Conserve energy.*
The body never leads the mind to ruin.
Therefore it is essential to discern between your choices.
Everything has its price.

19 *Play for the spirit.*
By playing for a motive, you will hold yourself back.
By accepting the simplicity of it all,
You will enter the Spirit of the game eternally.

20 *Strive for consistency.*
Lightning is commonplace; there is only one sun and one moon.
The real starting lineup you are up against is not out on the field,
But inside your heart;
At first base is Complacency,
At second, Anger,
At third, Fear,
At short, Fatigue,
Playing left field, Impatience,
In center, Pride,
In right, Jealousy,
Catching, Self-pity,
And warming up in the bull pen are Injury, Old Age, and Death.
If you can defeat this team, then you shall truly be World Champion
    and
Wear the ring of consistency.

THE TAO OF
UMPIRING

or It Ain't Nothing Till It's Called

An umpire is a perfect embodiment of the Tao.

He possesses both an equal measure of Yin, the earth, and Yang, heaven.

Too much Yang and he becomes domineering and loses sight of the game;

Too much Yin and he becomes hesitant and misses crucial calls.

Neutrality is thus a perfect balance between Yin and Yang, heaven and earth.

An umpire's effectiveness depends on his ability to balance the two.

And like the earth, he is trodden upon by everyone;

And like heaven, his judgments are absolute.

Like the earth, he supports everyone and favors no one;
Like heaven, he is always present, but only called upon in times of
need.

Like the earth, he abides by the letter of the law;
Like heaven, he is swift and ruthless in its enactment.

Like the earth, no one sings his praises;
Like heaven, everyone questions his calls.

Like the earth, he sees nothing;
Like heaven, he sees everything.

Like the earth, he is honest;
Like heaven, he is consistent.

Like the earth, he begins everything;
Like heaven, he ends everything.

And ultimately, like the earth, we cannot live without him;
And ultimately, like heaven, his decisions must be accepted.

THE TAO OF THE DESIGNATED HITTER

or It Takes Two to Tango

Take away the earth and what is heaven?
Take away woman and what is man?
Take away Yin and what is Yang?
Take away defense and what is offense?

Take away the bat from the pitcher and what is he when the
designated hitter comes to the plate?
Take away the glove from the designated hitter and what is he
when his team takes the field?

Incomplete.

A designated hitter is pure Yang with no Yin.
A pitcher with no bat is pure Yin with no Yang.
This goes against the laws of the Tao.
This goes against the Tao of the Game.
Does not every pitcher want to hit for his team?
Does not every designated hitter want to field?

Only the imbalanced support an imbalance.
Imbalance shall, nevertheless, always be restored to balance.
It is the law of the Tao.
Yin will be returned to Yang,
Yang will be returned to Yin,
The pitcher will hit,
The designated hitter will disappear like a fog in sunlight.

The Tao is at work in all things.

THE TAO OF NATURAL BASEBALL

Everything adapts to the times;
Everything must accept its fate.
Given the choice,
Everyone picks the natural before the artificial,
The clean over the dirty,
The new over the used,
The real over the phony.

And given the choice,
Everyone picks natural grass,
Day games,
Intimate ballparks, open to the sky,
The pitcher hitting,
Wooden bats.
Given the choice.

But if we have to,
We will accept and adapt to artificial turf,
Night games,
Large, impersonal domes,
The designated hitter,
And if it comes down to it, aluminum bats.

Given the choice.
And who determines that choice?
Everyone does.

THE TAO OF
THE
POLITICS OF
BASEBALL

Baseball is rooted in the Tao.
Anyone wanting to partake need only play;
Anyone wanting to watch need only look.
Because the game is always there, it remains timeless;
Because the game is all embracing, it is universal;
Because it asks nothing in return, we trust it;
Because it is fun to play, we love it.
When baseball is centered in the Tao,
The players play,
The fans turn out,
And the game takes care of itself.
Thus laws go unwritten and the leaders remain unknown.

When the league exerts its will upon the game,
The greater its ambition, the worse the results.
Try to influence the game and you destroy it;
Trying to satisfy the owners, the players suffer;
Trying to satisfy the players, the fans suffer;
Trying to satisfy the fans, the game suffers;
Trying to satisfy the game, the tradition suffers.
Therefore the best politics is no politics,
The best government is no government.
The wise commissioner puts the game above all else:
Abandoning the quantity of the profit,
The quality of the product will increase;
Abandoning the legislation of the game,
Mutual trust will be restored;
Abandoning the preservation of the game,
It will continue to flourish and grow.
He fulfills the needs of the game and empties its wants.
He restores the substance of the game and discards its appearance.
He protects all and not the few.
When baseball follows the Tao,
Players are signed because of merit and not because of race;

Managers are selected because of their leadership and not because
  of their politics.
When the Tao of baseball is strong,
Teams develop from within and loyalty is engendered.
When the Tao of baseball is weak,
Teams develop according to wealth and opportunism is instilled.
Patience and hard work produce a strong crop;
Reaping another man's labor produces ill will.
The Tao of baseball is thus strongest when it follows the Tao of
  Nature;
Everything changes according to need;
Fearing change, the game becomes prejudiced and insular and
  leads to decay;
Allowing change, the game becomes magnanimous and global and
  leads to prosperity.

The more powerful baseball becomes,
The greater the need to return to its original intent and spirit.
Losing sight of the original intent of "May the best team win," the
  game diminishes into a contest of individual egos.
Losing sight of the original spirit of playing ball, the game dimin-
  ishes into a contest of individual wealth.

Therefore,
To restore integrity and natural balance,
The wise man lets nature go its own way.
When the river exceeds its banks, there are floods;
What else can you do but wait for the waters to come down?
When the game exceeds its demand, teams fold;
When the league expands beyond the quality of its players, the
    caliber of play suffers;
When the costs exceed the income, the league deteriorates;
When love of money exceeds love of the game, corruption takes
    hold;
When the future of the game exceeds the present, there are players'
    strikes and lockouts.
The wise man takes things ahead by letting them return,
Sets about doing by undoing,
Heals by letting the illness run its course,
Changes by allowing things to change.
Those who try to control the game
And who protect their influence with segregation and money
Go against the spirit of the game.
They take from those who have little
And give to those who have too much.

They deprive the worthy
And nourish the unworthy.
Who cheers the loudest at the ballpark?
Who plays the hardest on the field?
Baseball was not created to be owned
Or to be an avenue to great fortune.
Loyalty cannot be bought,
Hearts cannot be purchased.
A good mother takes care of her children before herself.

If you want to find the wellspring,
Dig until you reach its source.

The fans follow the players,
The players follow the manager,
The manager follows the owner,
The owner follows the league,
The league follows the game,
The game follows the Tao.

If you want to find the summit,
Climb until you reach its peak.

The Tao leads the game,
The game leads the league,
The league leads the owner,
The owner leads the manager,
The manager leads the players,
The players lead the fans.

If you want to govern the game,
Place yourself below it.
If you want to lead the game,
You must learn how to follow it.

When the league prospers,
But the farm system loses money;
When owners spend money for top players
And not on building the team;
When players use their images for endorsements
And forget about their responsibilities to the young;
When the stadium is full of executives and the well to do
And the poor cannot afford admission,
All of this is far from the Tao of baseball.

If baseball is governed wisely,
Everyone will be content.
The fans will fill the ballparks,
The players will work hard at the game,
The owners will cover their costs.
Even though they can hear the cheering in nearby towns,
The fans will be content with their home team;
Even though a player is offered more money by another club,
He will be satisfied where he is;
Even though the owners turn a profit,
They will invest it back in the game;
Even though there are new technologies,
The tradition will stay the same.

THE TAO OF
ANCESTRAL
BASEBALL

Baseball follows the Tao.
It is born in the spring,
It matures in the summer,
It culminates in the fall,
It dies in the winter.
The stronger the sun, the longer it is played.

It is born in our youth,
It matures in our adolescence,
It culminates in our manhood,
It dies in our old age,
The stronger the will, the longer it is played.

Game is played after game,
Season after season,

The old reproduce the young,
The young supplant the old,
Generation after generation.

Upon this unending cycle,
Some will travel but a short way and beget few,
Others will travel close to the very end and beget many,
A few will travel beyond its limits and evolve a new breed.

And so,
Some will be quickly forgotten,
Others remembered for a long time,
And a few will never be forgotten.

The game may take place on the earth, but it is from the stars that we draw our inspiration. And what shall become of the game should the young forget the old, should men stop looking up to the stars? The longer you look into the heavens the more stars you see.

Should we lose sight of those guiding lights, baseball would lose its sense of direction; it would continue to change but without a strong purpose and would develop a lost generation. It is for this reason that tradition needs to be kept alive.

Many will point out the superiority of today's players and discard the past as worthless; many will point out the superiority of yesterday's players and discard the present. Both generations are necessary to each other, both support the other. The players of yesterday were as good as they could be, just as the players of today are as good as they can be, just as the players of tomorrow will be as good as they can be. We cannot compare one generation to the next to discover the best all-time players. Each player has benefited from those who have played before him. Each player stands to inherit more than those who have played before him.

Ancestral baseball must be kept alive directly, in the spirit of the players, in the knowledge that they are not the first ever to have played the game, nor will they be the last; that others have laid the Way for the present with nothing more than love and dedication for the game, and that playing the game in this generation is an honor, whose duty it is to keep alive the original spirit of the Ancestral players, whoever they may have been.

Everything is always as it should be. The Hall of Fame is not in Cooperstown. When we take to the field, it is right under our very feet and watching down upon us from the sky. If we can't see it, we will at least feel it. No one can completely forget the Tao.

THE TAO OF

BASEBALL

THE TAO OF
NO BASEBALL

The more you look, the more you see;
The more you see, the less you look.
The more you watch baseball, the more you understand;
The more you understand, the less you need to watch it.

In every moment, there is eternity.
Somewhere way out there and deep down inside,
Staring in at the catcher,
Rounding third base,
Hammering the ball deep into the seats,
Looking down upon that perfect green diamond,
Watching the game flicker on a TV screen on a hot summer night,
Rerunning games long finished in the vastness of remembrance,
In all those uncountable and unending moments,
Our experiences of the game begin to crystallize, and we can sense
    our own mortality and our own infinity. And we can witness our
    aloneness in this world.

And it is here that we see
That we play the game though there really is no game,
That we are proud of our team, though there really is no team,
That we compete though there is no opponent,
That we rush for the ball, though there are no outs,
That we race for the bag, though no one is safe,
That we slide into home, though there are no runs,
That we manage with every trick, though there is nothing to gain,
That we play by the rules, though there really are no rules,
That we root, root, root for the home team, though we are really
    alone in the stands,
That we wish "Fair" or "Foul," though the lines do not exist,
That we pay to attend and get paid to play, though the game has
    no real value,
That we cry "Safe" or "Out," though our judgment changes noth-
    ing,
That our hearts burst with joy, though nothing has really been won,
That our hearts break in pain, though nothing has really been lost,
That we love the game forever, though it does not really exist.

THE TAO OF
ONE BASEBALL

Therefore,

When everything hangs in the balance, and the game is on the
line,

Nine men on the field become one,

One man at the plate becomes the team,

The entire crowd becomes one fan,

The season comes down to one game,

The game to one inning,

The inning to one out,

The out to one pitch,

The win to one run,

Four bases to one plate,

The team to one player,

The league to one team,

The moment to one winner and one loser.

THE TAO OF
ABSOLUTE.
BASEBALL

And if we journey even further, we will come to a diamond
Where we shall see that
Everything is fair,
Nothing is foul,
Everybody is safe,
Nobody is out,
Everyone wins,
No one loses,
Everybody plays,
Nobody watches.

THE TAO OF BASEBALL, THE BASEBALL OF TAO

We understand according to our capacity.
Many have gone before us and many will come after us.
Each has something to give, something to add;
We augment each other's capacities.
Knowing what I know, I wish to add the Tao to Baseball.
Many will have a greater capacity for Baseball than I;
Many will have a greater capacity for the Tao than I;
My task has been to join the two together.

Baseball is like the Tao.
No one can understand it, therefore it is a mystery.
No one can predict its outcome, therefore it is full of possibilities.

It makes no demands, therefore we abide by it.

It forces no belief, therefore we have faith in it.

It costs nothing, therefore we give it our time.

It has no value, therefore we do not steal from it.

It gives back more than we put into it, therefore we cherish it.

It is silent, therefore we cheer it.

It is accountable, therefore we compile its statistics.

It is without attachments, therefore we forget our worries.

It is pure, therefore we teach it to our children.

It is fearless, therefore we are inspired by it.

It is humble, therefore we praise it.

It is selfless, therefore we see ourselves in it.

It is timeless, therefore we never tire of it.

It is always the same, therefore we improve at it.

It is always different, therefore we never master it.

It does not compete, therefore it challenges us.

It judges no one, therefore it is just.

It is egalitarian, therefore we all have a chance at it.

It has no limits, therefore we test ourselves in it.

It is ageless, therefore children take it up.

It does not take itself seriously, therefore we laugh at it.

It requires no effort, therefore it is full of grace.

It is of this world, therefore we practice it.
It is not of this world, therefore we dream about it.

The Tao is like baseball.
It does not distinguish between good and bad, rich or poor, big or
    little, young or old.
It knows no politics, geography, language, or race.
It is available everywhere,
And open to all mankind.

True baseball, like the Tao, is free.
Its only requirements are willing bodies, open space, a ball and a
    bat, and some gloves.
What you put into it determines what you take out.
If it were not free, children could not afford to play it.

After school is out and the work is done, we play.
No amount of money can make play into work.
We cannot eat baseballs; we cannot live at ballparks.
When the game is over or you are too old to play,
What shall you do?

And so like the game, this book has come down to one final inning,
   one final out.
Where has our game gotten us?
We have journeyed, and yet we have gone nowhere.
We know something and yet we understand even less.
What can we do?
Let go, give it everything we have, hang in tough at the plate.
Open our hearts to the Tao.

I have gone through my delivery and pitched.
The rest is up to you.

May you enter the Spirit,

GŌ

Who I Am

My mother gave birth to me on Turtle Island, in the city of Meeting Place, on the shores of Fine Lake (Toronto, Ontario). That's where I learned about baseball and that's where I learned about the Tao, among other things.

At heart I am a Yankee fan, but I root also for my home team, wherever that may be.

My name was given to me by my brother, D. Nkoma. It is simply a shortening of my Christian name to its first two letters. Coincidentally, in Japanese it means "work already done," and hence "karma." This is ironic, because in many ways I felt that I had already written this book before. It's about as good a reason as to why I wrote it.

At present, I reside in Meeting Place and am finishing a second book, *Do Cats Have the Buddha Nature?*